BEST JAVA PROGRAMS FOR BEGINNERS

PART - I

MD NABEEL

I would like to dedicate this book to My Parents,

Md Shakeeel and Nakhat Firdows,

and also to my Elder Brother,

Md Fuzail & My Siblings.

Contents

CHAPTER ONE

INTRODUCTION TO JAVA

JAVA was developed by James Gosling at Sun Microsystems Inc in the year 1995, later acquired by Oracle Corporation. It is a simple programming language. Java makes writing, compiling, and debugging programming easy. It helps to create reusable code and modular programs. Java is a class-based, object-oriented programming language and is designed to have as few implementation dependencies as possible. A general-purpose programming language made for developers to write once run anywhere that is compiled Java code can run on all platforms that support Java. Java applications are compiled to byte code that can run on any Java Virtual Machine. The syntax of Java is similar to c/c++.

History: Java's history is very interesting. It is a programming language created in 1991. James Gosling, Mike Sheridan, and Patrick Naughton, a team of Sun engineers known as the Green team initiated the Java language in 1991. Sun Microsystems released its first public implementation in 1996 as Java 1.0. It provides no-cost -run-times on popular platforms. Java1.0 compiler was re-written in Java by Arthur Van Hoff to strictly comply with its specifications. With the arrival of Java 2, new versions had multiple configurations built for different types of platforms.

In 1997, Sun Microsystems approached the ISO standards body and later formalized Java, but it soon withdrew from the process. At one time, Sun made most of its Java implementations available without charge, despite their proprietary software status. Sun generated revenue from Java through the selling of licenses for specialized products such as the Java Enterprise System.

On November 13, 2006, Sun released much of its Java virtual machine as free, open-source software. On May 8, 2007, Sun finished the process, making all of its JVM's core code available under open-source distribution terms.

The principles for creating java were simple, robust, secured, high performance, portable, multi-threaded, interpreted, dynamic, etc. In 1995 Java was developed by James Gosling, who is known as the Father of Java. Currently, Java is used in mobile devices, internet programming, games, e-business, etc.

CHAPTER TWO

PROGRAM 1

PROGRAM STATEMENT:

Write a Java program to print your Bio-data which includes your Name, Class, Subject, School and City.

ALGORITHIM:

STEP 1: Start the Program
STEP 2: Take variables
STEP 3: Give values to variables
STEP 4: Print statements including those variables
STEP 5: stop the Program

DATA DESCRIPTION TABLE:

VARIABLE NAME - DATA TYPE - PURPOSE/ FUNCTION
Name String To store a set of characters
Standard String To store a set of characters
Subject String To store a set of characters
School String To store a set of characters
City String To store a set of characters

PROGRAM CODING:

```java
// A sample program
public class Bio_Data
{
public static void main(String args[])
{
String Name="Md Nabeel";
String Standard="IX – A";
String Subject="Computer applications";
String School="Saifee Golden Jubilee Enghlih Public School";
String City="Kolkata";
System.out.println("Name: "+ Name);
System.out.println("Standard:"+ Standard);
System.out.println("Subject:"+ Subject);
```

```
System.out.println("School:"+ School);
System.out.println("City:"+ City);
}
}
```

OUTPUT:

Name: Md Nabeel
    Standard:IX – A
    Subject:Computer applications
    School:Saifee Golden Jubilee Enghlih Public School
    City:Kolkata

CHAPTER THREE

PROGRAM 2

PROGRM STATEMENT:

Write a program to showcase the way of printing in Java.

ALOGORITHIM:

STEP 1: Print some sentences in different lines.

DATA DESCRIPTION TABLE:

VARIABLE - DATA TYPE - PURPOSE
    s String To store a sentence

PROGRAM CODING:

```java
public class Java
    {
    public static void main (String args[])
    {
    String s= "Usage of print function";
    System.out.println(s);
    System.out.println("Introduction to Java Programming on BlueJ Platform");
    System.out.println("Java is an Object-Oriented Programming Language");
    System.out.println("Java Language is developed by James Gosling");
    System.out.println("This Language was initially called as Oak");
    System.out.println("Welcome to Java Programming");
    System.out.println("Enjoy Learning! ! ! !");
    }
    }
```

OUTPUT:

Introduction to Java Programming on BlueJ Platform
    Java is an Object-Oriented Programming Language
    Java Language is developed by James Gosling
    This Language was initially called as Oak

Welcome to Java Programming
Enjoy Learning ! ! ! !

CHAPTER FOUR

PROGRAM 3

PROGRM STATEMENT:

Write a program to create different objects through methods.

ALOGORITHIM:

STEP 1: Create three classes, each containing a method to print a tagline and the price
STEP 2: Declare the main class and create objects of the three classes.
STEP 3: Call the methods of the class using respective objects in order to print the data.

DATA DESCRIPTION TABLE:

VARIABLE - DATA TYPE - PURPOSE
Car1. object. Object of a class
Car2. object. Object of a class
Car3. object. Object of a class

PROGRAM CODING:

```
class RollsRoyce
    {
    public void price()
    {
    System.out.println("Rolls Royce is the king of cars");
    System.out.println("It's starting price is 6.25 crores in India");
    }
    }
    class Mercedes
    {
    public void price()
    {
    System.out.println("The Founder of Mercedes was Karl Benz");
    System.out.println("It's starting price is 40 lakhs in India");
    }
    }
    class BMW
```

```
{
public void price()
{
System.out.println("The Full form of BMW is Belgium Motor Works");
System.out.println("It's starting price is 40 lakhs in India");
}
}
public class Objects
{
public static void main()
{
RollsRoyce Car1 = new RollsRoyce();
Mercedes Car2 = new Mercedes();
BMW Car3 = new BMW();
Car1.price();
Car2.price();
Car3.price();
}
}
```

OUTPUT:

Rolls Royce is the king of cars
    It's starting price is 6.25 crores in India
    The Founder of Mercedes was Karl Benz
    It's starting price is 40 lakhs in India
    The Full form of BMW is Belgium Motor Works
    It's starting price is 40 lakhs in India

CHAPTER FIVE

PROGRAM 4

PROGRM STATEMENT:

Write a program to showcase the concept of objects as an instance of class.

ALOGORITHIM:

STEP 1: Create the first object of the class, and initialize the instance variables
STEP 2: Print the name of the car as the most stunning car of 2020 and its price in different lines.
STEP 3: Create the second object of the class, and initialize the instance variables
STEP 4: Print the name of the car as the most stunning car of 2020 and its price in different lines.

DATA DESCRIPTION TABLE:

VARIABLE. DATA TYPE PURPOSE
Price. int. To store the value of price of vehicle
Brand name int. To store the brand name of the vehicle

PROGRAM CODING:

```
class vehicle
    {
    int price;
    String brand_name;
    public static void main(String args[])
    {
    vehicle lamborghini =new vehicle();
    lamborghini.price=25000000;
    lamborghini.brand_name="Lamborghini Continental GT";
    System.out.println("The most stunning Vehicle of 2020 is "+lamborghini.brand_name);
    System.out.println("The price of "+ lamborghini.brand_name+ "is " +lamborghini.price);
    vehicle Tesla=new vehicle();
    Tesla.price=5000000;
    Tesla.brand_name="Cyber Truck";
    System.out.println("The most stunning Vehicle of 2020 is "+Tesla.brand_name);
    System.out.println("The price of "+ Tesla.brand_name+ "is " +Tesla.price);
    }
```

}

OUTPUT:

The most stunning Vehicle of 2020 is Lamborghini Continental GT
    The price of Lamborghini Continental GTis 25000000
    The most stunning Vehicle of 2020 is Cyber Truck
    The price of Cyber Truckis 5000000

CHAPTER SIX

PROGRAM 5

PROGRM STATEMENT:

A shopkeeper sells an article for Rs.10,000. If the rate of tax under GST is 10%, calculate and display the tax and the amount paid by the customer.

ALOGORITHIM:

STEP 1: Calculate the 10% GST
STEP 2: Calculate the final amount by adding GST to the principal price.
STEP 3: Print the total amount and GST levied.

DATA DESCRIPTION TABLE:

VARIABLE. DATA TYPE. PURPOSE
pr. int To store the value of principal cost
gst double To store the gst tax
amt double To store the final amount

PROGRAM CODING:

```java
// A Program to Calculate GST
public class GST
{
public static void main(String args[])
{
int p = 10270;
double g,a;
g = 10270*10.0/100.0*1;
a = p – g;
System.out.println("GST = " + g);
System.out.println("Amount to pay = " + a);
}
}
```

OUTPUT:

GST = 1027.0
    Amount to pay = 9243.0

CHAPTER SEVEN

PROGRAM 6

PROGRM STATEMENT:

A dealer allows his customer two successive discounts of 20% and 10%. If the article costs Rs. 7,200, calculate an display the selling price and the total discount given by the dealer.

ALGORITHIM:

STEP 1: Calculate the 20% discount and the next 10% discount.
STEP 2: Calculate the total discount and amount by the formula
STEP 3: Print the total discount and amount

DATA DESCRIPTION TABLE:

VARIABLE DATA TYPE PURPOSE
cp int To store the value of cp
d1 double To store 20% discount
d2 double To store the next 10% discount
dis double To store the value of the discount
amt double To store the value of the amount

PROGRAM CODING:

```java
// A program to Calculate discounts
public class Discount
{
public static void main(String args[])
{
int cp=7200;
double d1,d2,dis,amt;
d1=cp*20.0/100.0;
d2=(cp – d1)*10.0/100.0;
dis=d1 + d2;
amt=cp – dis;
System.out.println("Total Discount = "+ dis);
```

```
System.out.println("Total Amount = "+ amt);
}
}
```

OUTPUT:

```
Total Discount = 2016.0
    Total Amount = 5184.0
```

CHAPTER EIGHT

PROGRAM 7

PROGRAM STATEMENT:

In a class of 'n' number of students the number of girls is 'm'. Write a program to input the numbers n & m. Find and display the percentage of girl and boys in the class.

ALGORITHIM:

STEP 1: Get the number of students in class
    STEP 2: Get the number of girls in class.
    STEP 3: calculate the number of boys in class.
    STEP 4: Calculate their respective percentages
    STEP 5: Print the calculated answer

DATA DESCRIPTION TABLE:

VARIABLE. DATA TYPE PURPOSE
    n int To store the number of students
    m int To store the value of number of girls
    b int To store the value of number of boys
    perb Double To store the value of percentage of boys
    perg Double To store the value of percentage of girls

PROGRAM CODING:

```
import java.io.*;
    class percentage
    {
    public static void main(String args[])throws IOException
    {
    InputStreamReader read = new InputStreamReader(System.in);
    BufferedReader in = new BufferedReader(read);
    int n,m,b;
    double perb,perg;
    System.out.println("Enter number of Students and girls: ");
    n=Integer.parseInt(in.readLine());
    m=Integer.parseInt(in.readLine());
```

```
b=n-m;
perb=(double)b/n*100;
perg=(double)m/n*100;
System.out.println("Percentage of Boys = " + perb);
System.out.println("Percentage of Girls = "+ perg);
}
}
```

OUTPUT:

```
Enter number of Students and girls:
    250
    130
    Percentage of Boys = 48.0
    Percentage of Girls = 52.0
```

CHAPTER NINE

PROGRAM 8

PROGRAM STATEMENT:

Write a program in Java to accept the number of days and display it after converting into number of years, months and days.

ALGORITHIM:

STEP 1: Get the number of days to be converted
   STEP 2: calculate the number of years, months and days by dividing with 365 and then the remainder with 30 respectively
STEP 3: Print the calculated answer

DATA DESCRIPTION TABLE:

VARIABLE. DATA TYPE. PURPOSE
   a int To store the value of input days
   y int To store the value of number of years
   b int To store the value of number of remaining days after years
   c int To store the value of number of months
   d int To store the value of number of days

PROGRAM CODING:

```
import java.io.*;
    public class days
    {
    public static void main(String args[])throws IOException
    {
    int a,b,c,y,d;
    InputStreamReader read = new InputStreamReader(System.in);
    BufferedReader in = new BufferedReader(read);
    System.out.println("Enter number of days: ");
    a = Integer.parseInt(in.readLine());
    y = a/365;
    b = a%365;
    c = b/30;
```

```
d = b%30;
System.out.println("The no. of years: " + y);
System.out.println("The no. of months: "+ c);
System.out.println("The no. of days: " + d);
}
}
```

OUTPUT:

```
Enter number of days:
    1027
    The no. of years: 2
    The no. of months: 9
    The no. of days: 27
```

CHAPTER TEN

PROGRAM 9

PROGRAM STATEMENT:

Write a program in Java to find and display the diagonal of a square taking side of the squareas an input.

ALGORITHIM:

STEP 1: Get the numeric value of the side of a square
STEP 2: Apply the formula and calculate the diagonal of the square using the given input
STEP 3 : Print the calculated answer

DATA DESCRIPTION TABLE:

VARIABLE DATA TYPE. PURPOSE
a int To store the value of the side of the square
d double To store the value of the diagonal of the square

PROGRAM CODING:

```
// A program to find the diagonal of a square
import java.util.*;
public class S_Diagonal
{
public static void main(String args[])
{
Scanner in = new Scanner(System.in);
int a;
double d;
System.out.println("Enter the side of the Square ");
a=in.nextInt();
d=Math.sqrt(2)*a;
System.out.println("Side of square = " + a);
System.out.println("Diagonal of square = " + d);
}
}
```

OUTPUT:

Enter the side of the Square
    50
    Side of square = 50
    Diagonal of square = 70.71067811865476

PROGRAM 10

PROGRM STATEMENT:

The final velocity of a vehicle can be calculated by using the formula:

$(v2 = u2 + 2as)$;

where u = initial velocity, a = acceleration, s = distance covered.

Write a Java program to calculate and display the final velocity by taking the initial velocity, acceleration and the distance covered as inputs.

ALOGORITHIM:

STEP 1: Get the numeric value of initial velocity

STEP 2: Get the numeric value of acceleration

STEP 3: Get the numeric value of distance covered

STEP 4: Apply the formula and calculate the final velocity with the given input.

STEP 5: Print the Final velocity

DATA DESCRIPTION TABLE:

VARIABLE. DATA TYPE PURPOSE

u. int To store the value of initial velocity

a int To store the value of acceleration

s int To store the value of distance coved

v double To calculate and display the final velocity

PROGRAM CODING:

```java
// A program to calculate the Final Velocity
import java.util.*;
public class F_Velocity
{
public static void main(String args[])
{
Scanner in = new Scanner(System.in);
int u,a,s;
double v;
System.out.println("Enter Initial Velocity: ");
```

```
u = in.nextInt();
System.out.println("Enter Acceleration: ");
a = in.nextInt();
System.out.println("Enter the distance covered: ");
s = in.nextInt();
v = Math.sqrt(Math.pow(u,2)+ 2*a*s);
System.out.println("The Final velocity is: " + v);
}
}
```

OUTPUT:

Enter Initial Velocity:
   40
Enter Acceleration:
   50
Enter the distance covered:
   200
The Final velocity is: 146.9693845669907

Why Sholud We Learn Java ?

10 REASONS TO LEARN JAVA ARE :

Java is a general-purpose, object-oriented programming language that was designed by James Gosling at Sun Microsystems in 1991. The compilation of the Java applications results in the bytecode that can be run on any platform using the Java Virtual Machine. Because of this, Java is also known as a WORA (Write Once, Run Anywhere) language. In modern times, Java is one of the most popular programming languages as it can be used to design customized applications that are light and fast and serve a variety of purposes. According to the TIOBE Index for April 2022, Java is among the top three programming languages.

Moving down, you will find the top 10 reasons that will elaborate on why to learn Java.

1. Java's Popularity and High Salary

Java is one of the most popular programming languages in the world. It is used by some 9 million developers and it runs on around 7 billion devices worldwide according to Oracle blogs. Because of the high demand for Java, Java developers are also quite sought after and they hold some of the most high-paying jobs in the industry. The average salary of a Java Developer lies between $47,169 to $106,610 per year.

2. Java is Easy to Learn

Java is quite easy to learn and can be understood in a short span of time as it has a syntax similar to English. You can also follow Java Tutorials. This will guide you on how to get started with Java and make yourself proficient in it.

3. Java has a Large Community

There is a large online community of Java users ranging from beginner, intermediate, and even expert levels that are particularly helpful in case any support is required. Also, GeeksforGeeks provides you with the best resource for Java.

4. Java has an Abundant API

Java has an abundant Application Programming Interface (API) that includes many Java classes, packages, interfaces, etc. This is useful for constructing applications without necessarily knowing their inside implementations. Java has mainly three types of API i.e. Official Java core APIs, Optional official Java APIs, and Unofficial APIs. These APIs overall are used for almost everything including networking, I/O, databases, media, XML parsing, speech synthesis, etc.

Now you have a great opportunity to learn Java from scratch! Yes with GeeksforGeeks Java Programming Foundation – Self Paced course for beginners that gives you clarification about every concept of language.

5. Java has Multiple Open Source Libraries

Open-source libraries have resources that can be copied, studied, changed, shared, etc. There are multiple open source libraries in Java such as JHipster, Maven, Google Guava, Apache Commons, etc. that can be used to make Java development easier, cheaper and faster.

6. Java has Powerful Development Tools

There are many Integrated development environments (IDEs) in Java that provide various facilities for software development to programmers. Powerful Java IDEs such as Eclipse, NetBeans, IntelliJ IDEA, etc. play a big role in the success of Java. These IDEs provide many facilities such as debugging, syntax highlighting, code completion, language support, automated refactoring, etc. that make coding in Java easier and faster. Java has created a base for the Android operating system and opted around 90% of fortune 500 companies to develop a lot of back-end applications. Also, it plays a great role in Apache Hadoop data processing, Amazon Web Services, Windows Azure, etc.

7. Java is Free of Cost

One of the reasons Java is very popular among individual programmers is that it is available under the Oracle Binary Code License (BCL) free of charge. This means that Java is free for development and test environments, but for commercial purposes, a little pay is required.

8. Java is Platform Independent

Java is platform-independent as the Java source code is converted to byte code by the compiler which can then be executed on any platform using the Java Virtual Machine. Java is also known as a WORA (write once, run anywhere) language because it is platform-independent. Also, the development of most Java applications occurs in a Windows environment while they are run on a UNIX platform because of the platform-independent nature of Java.

9. Java has Great Documentation Support

The documentation support for Java is excellent using Javadoc which is the documentation generator for Java. It uses the Java source code to generate the API documentation in HTML format. So, Javadoc provides a great reference while coding in Java so that understanding the code is quite simple.

10. Java is Versatile

Java is very versatile as it is used for programming applications on the web, mobile, desktop, etc. using different platforms. Also, Java has many features such as dynamic coding, multiple security features, platform-independent characteristics, network-centric designing, etc. that make it quite versatile. It doesn't matter if you are in high school or are in the first year of your college, if you have the curiosity to learn to code, today is the day to start.